BEAUCOUP

BANDANAS

Sara A. Shaw

50 Plus Creative Ways
TO USE BANDANAS AS AN EXPERIENTIAL
TOOL IN THE CLASSROOM, IN THE GYM
OR AT CAMP

Copyright© 2005 by Sara Shaw
ISBN 0-9646541-8-0
Learning Unlimited Corporation
5155 East 51st, Suite 108
Tulsa, OK 74135
(918) 622-3292 fax (918) 622-4203
Printed in the United States of America

In Loving Memory
of
Tamara Renee Chavous

August 29, 1984 - August 12, 2003

Loving Friend, Mentor, Sister, Daughter, and
Friend to all Children.

About The Book:

Beaucoup Bandanas is not a book you should try to read from start to finish. This book was designed to be a quick reference guide for anyone who needs something fun and simple to get a group moving and mixing. Inside you will find activities for all ages ranging from quick icebreakers to dynamic activities.

<u>Some bandana rules:</u>
1. Do not use bandanas to snap your partner or team mates.
2. Do not use these bandanas to blow your nose on.
3. Do not tie these bandanas to your clothing.
4. Wash your bandanas after every use. Use Hypo Allergenic detergent and no fabric softeners because some people have sensitive skin.
5. If someone is uncomfortable with being blindfolded do not force the issue.
6. If you choose to have your team or group wear bandanas on their heads do not inter change bandanas due to health concerns such as lice.
7. Recycle your torn bandanas.
8. All stained bandanas should be thrown away.
9. If a bandana becomes soiled with blood or any other bodily fluid discard in proper hazardous waste bin. Remember to wear gloves.
10. When playing tail tag make sure bandanas are not shoved all the way into pockets or waist bands. If this happens these bandanas should be taken out of play because they should be considered dirty.
11. Do not use "Ragger Program Bandanas." (Kids and adults can participate and earn up to seven different rags by doing good deeds in Ragger Program.)

***Please be aware of what type of bandanas you use. Depending on your location it may matter what color of bandana you use and what type of design is on the bandana.**

Special Thanks to:

ACA Basic Camp Director Course Participants from
    April 6 – 10, 2003
Camp Alexander, Emporia, KS
Nikki Campbell and Trevor Yakel of Camp Alexander
Carol J. Krueger, Prudential Emporia Realtors, Emporia, KS
*Dr. Glen Lojka, Manhattan, KS
Gridley Elementary School, Gridley, KS
Logan Avenue School, Emporia, KS
*Luke Austenfeld, Sherman Lake YMCA, Augusta, MI
JCYS Camp Henry Horner, Ingleside, IL
Kenny Allen of Mosey Outdoor Adventure Society, Wichita, KS
Khristin Morgan, Camp Alexander, Emporia, KS
Olpe Elementary and High School, Olpe, KS
Reading Elementary School, Reading KS
Sarah Crooks, Emporia KS
Cory Cannon
ESU Faculty (Dr. Joella Mehrhof, Dr. Kathy Ermler, and Dr.
    Clint D. Longacre)
Donna Tate and Sam Sikes for publishing help
Thomas A. Krueger my father and lawyer
My husband Dr. Rodney Shaw for keeping me moving and my
    4 children, Tamara, Katelin, Audree, and Erik, for being my
    inspiration.
Mickey Smith and Chrystal Carmann for always being there
    with a helping hand and anyone else I may have forgotten.

I also would like to thank God for granting me another chance.
    (In 1992 I suffered a severe head injury and almost died
    but, by God's grace I lived to play another day.)

* indicates my mentors.

Contents

Chapter I

Mixers / Ice Breakers /
Get to Know You Games

Chapter II

Initiatives

Chapter III
Group Games

Chapter IV
Bandanas on the Ropes Course

Chapter One

Mixers

Ice Breakers

Get To Know You Games

Laugh Out Loud

Sequence:
Ice Breakers

Activity Energy Level:
Medium to High

Group Size:
20+

Equipment Needed:
One or more bandanas depending on size of the group

Objective:
To get a group to warm up and to liven up.

Playing the Game:
Ask the group to form a large circle and number off by twos. Next have the twos step forward and face the ones. The twos should be about two arm lengths away from the ones. The object is to laugh as the bandana(s) are being tossed from one person to the next. Tossing must be done to someone across from you not next to you. If a bandana falls, the group must go silent until the bandana is picked back up and put into play. The groups yell "bandana down" to let everyone in the group know there is a bandana down and silence is needed.

Variations:
Substitute soft laughs, snickers, high pitched laughs, low belly laughs, or silence until a bandana hits the ground then one big HA!

Debriefing Topics:
- How did you feel when you were laughing out loud?
- If you felt silly, why is it okay to feel silly while we play together?
- What problems did your group run into when playing this game?
- Can you think of another fun way to play this game?

Create a Rainbow

Sequence:
Ice Breaker

Activity Energy Level:
Low to Medium

Group Size:
10+ (if you have a large group divide them into smaller sizes and make it a contest)

Equipment Needed:
Bandanas for everyone in assorted colors.

Objective:
Have the group create a rainbow using the bandanas in the most creative way. The object is to come up with multiple ideas. Be creative.

*** *I would recommend not letting your group tie the bandanas together. This can make it hard to untie for other activities.*

Variations:
Create the rainbow on the ground without letting bandanas lose human contact, or make it so that each person has to hold his or her own bandana with two hands, not allowing it to be touched by any other bandana or the ground.

*** The possibilities are limited only by the participants' imagination and the facilitators' rules. You can make it as difficult as needed.

Debriefing Topics:
- How did you feel when you had to work so close to each other?
- If you had to do this over would you change anything?
- What limitations did you run into?
- Did you feel that everyone listened to each other's ideas?

Matchmaker

Sequence:
Getting to Know You

Activity energy level:
Medium

Group size:
20+

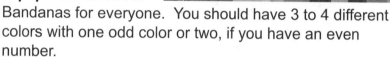

Equipment needed:
Bandanas for everyone. You should have 3 to 4 different colors with one odd color or two, if you have an even number.

The objective:
To get to know each other

Playing the game:
Have everyone grab a blindfold out of a bag and blindfold themselves. One or two people will get an odd color (Depending on group size). The facilitator then walks up to the one or two people with the odd colors and removes each of their blindfolds. These one or two people become the Matchmakers. They will pair up same color bandanas and have them stand back to back. The facilitator then asks a question that must be answered by both people in each pair. (e.g., What is your favorite food, animal, color, soft drink, etc.)? Then the pairs get to guess who they are paired with. If no one guesses correctly they may ask each other another yes or no question until a pair guesses the other person's name. Once a pair guesses who the other is, they take off their

blindfolds and give them to the Matchmaker(s), who takes their place and play begins again.

Variations:
While playing, the Matchmakers and facilitator need to act as spotters and referees. The facilitator's role is to let the Matchmakers lead as much of the activity as possible. Remember to ask only simple, general questions since this is a mixer. When working with a group later on in a program, harder, more sharing questions, can be used to make this a trust/cooperative game.

Debriefing topics:
- What did it feel like to be the Matchmaker?
- When you had to guess who you were paired with how did you feel?
- How did you deal with any problems that came up while playing this game?

Odd Man Out

Sequence:
Mixer

Activity energy level:
Medium

Group size:
20+

Equipment needed:
Enough bandanas for everyone minus the number of groups you need. (e.g., 30 people- need 3 groups of 10. (30 – 3) So you'll need 27 bandanas, 9 blue, 9 red, 9 yellow)
.

The objective:
To get to know each other and raise awareness on being the Odd Man Out.

Playing the game:
Throw all the bandanas in the center. Ask the group to run in and grab a bandana. Of course 3 people will end up without a bandana. Now have each of the same-colored groups adopt an Odd Man Out. Have the group interview that person. Then have each group introduce the person they interviewed. Now throw the bandanas back in the middle and start again.

Challenge:
To learn how to interview a person and introduce them. We want everyone to feel comfortable and safe when he or she plays — so be nice.

Variations:
Smaller groups, or have the Odd Man Out interview the group and then introduce the group.

Debriefing topics:
- How did it feel not to get a bandana?
- How did you like being asked questions by a group?
- How did it feel to be introduced?

Group Builder

Sequence:
Mixer/Splitting groups up for activities

Activity energy level:
Low to Medium

Group size:
12+

Equipment needed:
2 or 3 different colored bandanas with enough to make pairs for everyone. For example, if you want to end up with two groups of six then you only need 6 red and 6 blue.

The objective:
To find a partner who has the same color bandana as yourself. Then share three things with that person. (e.g., favorite color, middle name, favorite movie).

Playing the game:
Hand out bandanas to the group. Each person gets only the one you give them. (Best friends will usually pick the same color.)

Next have the group find someone who has the same color as they do. (Allow groups of two only, unless there are an odd number of participants.) Have them share three things, then find another pair who has the same color as they do. Once this is done have them ask questions and share. Continue the activity until you have the group size you want.

Variations:
Have each person find another person who has the same colored bandana and has one other thing in common with them. Then have that pair find another pair who has something in common with them.

Debriefing topics:
- For those of you who did not find a partner right away how did you feel?
- What was the "coolest" thing that you had in common with your partner?
- What did you learn from this activity?
- How can use what you learned from this activity in everyday life?

Bandana Group Juggle

Sequence:
Mixer

Activity energy level:
Medium to high

Group size:
8-12

Equipment needed:
Bandana scraps tied into balls, knots, dolls, or odd shapes

The objective:
To toss the object or objects around to people in the circle, in the same order without dropping the object so that everyone learns each other's names.

Playing the game:
Form a circle including the facilitator. Go around the circle and yell your first name. Next the facilitator tosses an object to someone across the circle making eye contact with that person and saying that person's name before tossing the object.

***Note: Everyone gets the object only once.

If an object is dropped, start over at the beginning. The game should end with the facilitator receiving the object from the last person in the group to catch the object.

Sometimes it helps to have the group put their hands behind their backs once they have received and thrown the first object.

Variations:
See how fast a group can go without dropping the object. (My record is a group of 15 that did it in one second). Pass multiple objects in multiple orders. Say the name of the person and what it is you are passing. (e.g., "Julie Blue Bandana Ball.") Then pass the blue bandana ball.

Debriefing topics:
- What did you see as your group progressed through this activity?
- Why were most of the mistakes made?

Bandana Grab Bag

Sequence:
Ice Breaker

Activity Energy Level:
Low to Medium

Group Size:
10+

Equipment Needed:
One bag that you can't see through. Bandanas for everyone in assorted colors making sure they are in pairs.

Objective:
Pair up and share.

Playing the game:
To start have each person step forward and draw a bandana from the bag and find his or her match. Have them introduce themselves and share one or two things about themselves. Put the bandanas back in the bag and go again. Do this a few more times making sure they ask different questions each time. (You may want to facilitate the questions.) I normally only do this three times and then have the group stand in a circle. Starting with the person on the left, find out who interviewed them and have those people step forward and tell the group about that person. This continues around the circle until everyone has been introduced.

Variations:
Have the group interview their matches in a non-verbal manner. (e.g., using hand signals, or by body movements). Pick the interview questions (e.g., Favorite Color, Favorite Food, Number of siblings in your family.) At the end of the interview rotations have people pair up with their first-question people and then do introductions.

Debriefing Topics:
- How did it feel to answer these questions?
- Did any of you find something in common with the people you interviewed?
- If you were to see one of the people you interviewed later, do you think you would at least remember the details they shared with you?
- What did you feel when you were being introduced?
- Is it okay to feel that way? Why is it okay?

Quick Skits

Sequence:
Mixer

Activity energy level:
Low to medium

Group size:
8+

Equipment needed:
Bandanas, slips of paper with topics on each slip, miscellaneous objects small enough to fit inside of a bandana

The objective:
To help a group to mix with each other and be creative.

Game preparation:
Take the bandanas and lay them flat in separate areas. Place three to five objects and a slip of paper with a topic on it on each bandana. Tie up each bandana into a bundle. Make sure you have enough bundles for however many groups you have.

Playing the game:
Split your group into smaller groups of three to six. Have each group pick a bundle. Give each group about 10-15 minutes to plan a skit. After the time is up, have the small group present their skit to the rest of the group.

Variations:
Have the skits performed non-verbally. Have the group guess what the skit is about.

Debriefing topics:
- How did your group decide who was doing what?
- What was the hardest thing for your group?
- How did your group overcome this obstacle?

Same/Same

Sequence:
Ice Breaker

Activity Energy Level:
Low to Medium

Group Size:
10+

Equipment Needed:
Enough bandanas of the same color and permanent markers for everyone.

Objective:
To get each person to know two people really well and for them to have a group to work with for the day, weekend, or week.

Playing the game:
Give everyone a bandana and have them find someone in the group who has one thing in common with them. Ask that pair to put their names on each other's bandana stating what it was they had in common. Next, ask the group to do this one more time finding a new partner who has something very unusual in common with them. (e.g., broke the same bone, same birthday, drive the same make and year of car, etc.) To end the game, have each person look at the different names on their bandana. Explain that the two people listed on their bandana are their buddies for the conference, or group activity.

Variations:
Have the first pair find a second pair with something in common with them. You could then have that group find another group and so on until you have the whole group as one big group.

Debriefing Topics:
- Did you find someone right away in the beginning that had something in common with you?
- Was it difficult to find something in common?
- How did you feel when you explored each other's life to find that special something?

Birthday Line and Positive Traits

Sequence:
Mixer

Activity energy level:
Medium

Group size:
12+

Equipment needed:
Multicolored bandanas

The objective:
To line up in birth date order while blindfolded and not talking. Once this is done, have your line circle up and then share one positive trait about them that starts with the same letter as their color of bandana. (e.g., Red=Ready to learn).

Playing the game:
Give everyone in your group a bandana. Ask everyone in your group to put on a blindfold. Next, have the group form a line according to birthdays. January 1 at one end and December 31 at the other. Tell the group to do this without talking. (However, if they are younger, go ahead and allow talking.) Once the group is lined up they will signal to you, without talking, that they are done. Next have the participants remove their blindfolds and check their work. Once you have checked their work, ask the line to move around to form a circle. Have each participant look at his/her bandana and come up with a

positive trait about themself that starts with the same
letter as the color of his/her bandana.

Variations:
Do not use the blindfolds for the positive traits, have
participants come up with their own positive trait. Only
blindfold half the group for the lineup and allow them to
talk, do not allow the non-blindfolded people to talk.
Have participants group up with the same colored
bandanas and come up with a common positive group
trait.

Debriefing topics:
- How did the group decide what to do first?
- When you could not talk or see what were you thinking?
- What worked for the group?
- What did not work?

Bandana Monster

Sequence:
Mixer/ Ice Breakers

Activity energy level:
Medium

Group size:
12+

Equipment needed:
At least two bandanas for each person and anything else you may have lying around.

The objective:
To get the whole to be creative and work together.

Playing the game:
Ask participants get into groups of at least five. Each group gathers two bandanas per person. The group is instructed to create a monster using every bandana their team has and every team member. The groups are also allowed to use objects in the room. The groups must create a monster and come up with a name and story about their monster.

Variations:
You can set time limits for the entire group for preparation time and presentation time. Give the participants paper and a writing utensil so they can write a good story.

Debriefing topics:
- What problems did your group run into when creating your monster?
- How did you overcome those problems?
- What can you take with you from this activity for rest of the day?

Beaucoup Bandanas

Chapter Two

Initiatives

Circle Flip

Sequence:
Initiatives

Activity Energy Level:
Low

Group Size:
10+

Equipment Needed:
Bandanas for everyone in assorted colors.

Objective:
Have the group form a circle with bandanas in between them so that instead of holding hands they are holding on to the bandanas. Tell the group they need to turn the circle inside out so that everyone is facing with their back to the inside of the circle. They must do this without letting go and without twisting themselves.

Variations:
Have the group form two circles that intertwine and have them flip both circles.

Debriefing Topics:
- Did you feel that everyone listened to each other's ideas?
- Do you feel that as a group you need to set rules or boundaries for your team before continuing today?

Skin the Bandana

Sequence:
Initiatives

Activity energy level:
Medium to High

Group size:
12+

Equipment needed:
Bandanas for everyone

The objective:
To line up and flip the line without letting go

Playing the game:
Ask everyone get one bandana and hold it in his or her right hand. Then have everyone line up in a straight line, legs spread apart. Next, have everyone put their right hand (holding the bandana) between their legs. Have the person behind them grab the person's bandana in front of them with their left hand. Once everyone is set up, tell the group that, without stepping over the bandana in the front of them and behind them and without letting go, they must get the person in front of the line to the back of the line.

Do not allow the players to just walk around the flip the line.

Variations:
Do not allow the group to crawl forward through legs. Have them end with the bandanas still between their legs. Blindfold a couple of people or half the group.

Debriefing topics:
- What did you think?
- Was it hard to crawl through the line?
- How did you manage to stay attached?
- Why did your line not stay hooked?
- Or, why did your line stay hooked up?

Hot Spots

Sequence:
Initiatives

Activity energy level:
Medium

Group size:
5+

Equipment needed:
A long rope and lots of bandanas, balls, cones, bandana dolls, or any other objects to act as hot spots.

The objective:
To navigate each player down the path without touching or stepping on a hot spot.

Playing the game:
Set the rope up in a winding path. Put the bandanas, balls, and miscellaneous items in this pathway leaving only a few spots to step. Next, explain to the group that they need to navigate the pathway while blindfolded. No one else can step in the path except the blindfolded person.

Variations:
Allow no talking. Blindfold the person giving commands as the person walking the path.

Debriefing topics:
- What did you feel when you were blindfolded?
- How did it feel to be the leader?
- Was there anything you would have done different during the game?

Color Touch

Sequence:
Initiative

Activity energy level:
Medium

Group size:
5+

Equipment needed:
Bandanas of different colors.

The objective:
To lead the blindfolded group to a certain color.

Playing the game:
Everyone is given a different colored bandana. Everyone knows their own color. Ask each person to put on his or her blindfold. Next, have the group spread out by listening to your clues. (e.g., Yellow take 2 steps to the right, Red take 5 steps back).

When you have the group spread out, pick a leader by asking a certain color of bandana to take off their bandana. The leader is then given their first task. Everyone must touch green. The leader then must instruct the blindfolded people in the right direction so everyone is touching green. Once done, pick a new leader and have that leader spread back out and go again

Variations:
Have two leaders set up obstacles on the floor. Allow each person to move only 2 or 3 times

Debriefing topics:
- What was it like to be the leader?
- How did you feel moving and being blindfolded?
- When your color was called and everyone had to touch you, how did you feel?

Team Tail Pinning

Sequence:
Initiative

Activity energy level:
Medium to high

Group size:
10 - 20

Equipment needed:
Blindfolds for the whole group and a stuffed animal or a taped outline of an animal.

The objective:
Guide your blindfolded group to the center and pin the tail on the stuffed animal or taped animal outlined on the floor or wall. Team that gets the closest to the objective wins.

Playing the game:
Split group into teams of 4 or 5. Have them line up with their group. Blindfold everyone except the person in back. Then, have the groups of 4 or 5 put their hands on each others shoulders creating a small line controlled by the back person.

As the back person steers the group to the center object, the front person holds the extra bandanas. The back person's job is to steer and direct the front person to pin the tail on the animal. The group must always stay together and attached.

Variations:
Allow the back person to steer only. The person may not talk. Insist that the line stays straight.

Debriefing topics:
- How did it affect the group having the leader in back?
- Do you think your team worked well together?
- Is there anything you learned playing this game that you could take with you?

Hook Up

Sequence:
Initiatives

Activity energy level:
Low

Group size:
12+

Equipment needed:
Bandanas for everyone.

The objective:
To get everyone to hook up into one big line or circle.
Everyone must be hooked up differently.

Playing the game:
Instruct the team, after giving each player a bandana, that
they must hook up to each other using the bandanas. The
only rule is that everyone must hook up differently. (e.g., The
first person by putting an end of their bandana in their pocket
and the other end in the pocket of the second person. The
second person must hook up to a third person some other
fashion). This continues until the group is finished. The
facilitator then checks out the group's handiwork.

Variations:
If the first person hooks his or her end of the bandana in his or
her pocket then the other end must be hooked to the next
person another way. No two people can be hooked together
in the same fashion. The group must end up in a circle with
everyone interconnected differently.

Debriefing topics:
- Was there any planning?
- Is it okay to do things by trial and error?
- If yes, why and when? If no, Why?

Human Knot

Sequence:
Initiatives

Activity energy level:
Medium

Group size:
12+

Equipment needed:
Bandanas for everyone.

The objective:
To knot up the group and then have the group untangle without letting go.

Playing the game:
Have each person hold their bandana in their right hand and then bunch together. Next have everyone put up both of their hands (with the bandana still in there right hand.) Ask each person to reach across the circle and grab hold of one end of someone else's bandana with their left hand. Have them lower their arms after they are holding two bandanas. Without letting go of the bandanas, they need to untwist this knot.

* *Important: Do not allow two people to hold on to each other's bandana. They must reach across the circle.*

Variations:
Tie the knot up according to birthdays. Start with January in the middle then work your way out to December.

Debriefing topics:
- What worked for the group when untwisting this knot?
- Do you feel your group was successful? Why or why not?
- How did you feel when you were that close to everyone?

Untie It

Sequence:
Initiative

Activity energy level:
Medium

Group size:
12+

Equipment needed:
A long rope and bandanas.

The objective:
To untie all the knots in the rope, as a group, while blindfolded

Playing the game:
Take a long rope and tie several knots in it. Lay it on the ground and have the group sit in a circle around the rope. Ask the group to study the knots but not touch the rope. Next, have the group blindfold themselves and pick up the rope. Everyone must be touching the rope at all times. Have the group work together to untie all the knots.

Variations:
For younger kids put only one or two knots in the rope. Instead of blindfolding the group tie the bandanas and rope in a knot. Then have the group untie the rope and untangle the bandanas ending with everyone having a bandana.

Debriefing topics:
- So what did you feel/think?
- How did you feel the group did?
- What do you think your group needs to do to succeed?

Planes, Trains & Automobiles

Sequence:
Initiatives

Activity energy level:
Medium

Group size:
24 + The more the better!

Equipment needed:
Different props such as bandanas, balls, noodles, chairs, broom, fabric scraps, etc.. Index cards. You decide how few or how many cards labeled with different types of planes, trains, and automobiles.

The objective:
One person from a group draws a piece of paper from a bandanna. Perhaps you draw "Taxi" for your group. Without telling the others in your group, you must relay this info to your group so they can pose for the remaining groups to guess what type of "plane, train, or automobile" your group represents

Playing the game:
Break the large groups into groups of 10 or more. One person from each group comes forward and draws an object out of a hat. Example: taxi, bus, semi, commercial airline, helicopter, passenger train, freight train, etc. Have fun making up your own. The person drawing must present this idea to their group without talking or writing it down. Once your group has established what they are to reenact, you may get the props from the center of the activity area. Without talking, your

group is to act out this plane, train, or automobile so that the other groups can guess what it is.

Variations:
More or fewer props. Blindfold everyone in the group except the runner and the creator. Allow talking in the groups.

Debriefing topics:
- How did your group communicate without words?
- Did the whole team understand what was going on?
- If not, what could have been done differently?
- If so, how did your group accomplish this?

Survivor

Sequence:
Initiatives

Activity energy level:
Medium

Group size:
24 + The more the better!

Equipment needed:
Rope, spot markers, raccoon circles, hula-hoops, and bandanas for each participant.

The objective:
To rescue your teammates from the islands and bring them back to the mainland.

Playing the game:
Create a Survivor Island with the rope. You can either section off an area or make a giant circle to be the Survivor Island. Place the raccoon circles, hula-hoops, and spot markers around the playing area to make smaller islands. Place The first hula hoop about 7 feet away from the Survivor Island. The rest of the little islands should be farther away than the first.

One of the spot markers needs to be placed on the Survivor Island to act as the anchor for the rescuing team. The rescue team consists of three people to start with. One person is the anchor and stands on the spot marker on the Survivor Island. The two other rescuers connect to the anchorperson by holding onto each other's bandanas forming a rescue line. The rescue line then visits the closest island rescuing one stranded person at a time by having the person connect to the rescuers by using a bandana. The person then rescued is brought back to the Survivor Island and becomes the anchor. While playing no one may let go of the bandanas. If this happens they could be swept out to sea to a far away island or to the place of the facilitator's choice. The only time anyone can let go of the bandanas is when they are back on Survivor Island. The game is completed when each person is rescued and returned to Survivor Island.

Variations:
Change the playing area with more or fewer islands. Give the group a time limit. Allow the group to create rescue lines from smaller island to smaller island.

Debriefing topics:
- How did your group communicate with being so spread out?
- Did the whole team understand what was going on?
- If not, what could have been done differently?
- If so, how did your group accomplish this?

Who's Got my Tail Remix
(Khristins' special)

Sequence:
Initiative

Activity energy level:
High

Group size:
10+

Equipment needed:
Bandanas for each player. Bouncy Balls, (Basket Balls work best). Open area with a hard surface so balls can be dribbled.

The objective:
To strengthen hand eye coordination and become more aware of people around you. Explore the possibility or working together to be the last person standing.

Playing the game:
Everyone is giving a bandana to put in his/her back pocket or in his/her waistband. The bandana needs to hang down almost to the back of the knees creating a tail. Please remember to review the bandana rules and set up the boundaries. Everyone is giving a basketball and then told to spread out. When the facilitator says "go" everyone starts dribbling his or her basketball and tries to steal others' bandanas. When you pull someone else's bandana either tuck it in your front pocket or put it over your shoulder. People are not allowed to steal these bandanas and they are not replacement bandanas if yours is stolen. They are kept as points only. When your tail is stolen you must sit down with your ball in your lap. Keep the bandanas you have because they count as points. You may still steal others bandanas when they run by. This would cause that person to have to sit

down. You only get another point. The last person standing and the person with the most bandanas win.

Variations:
If you are playing this with younger children I suggest using smaller balls like tennis balls that the child must hold in one hand. Then if the ball is dropped or their tail is stolen then the child must sit out. For older more experienced players partner people up and have them do bounce passing while trying to steal others' tails. Divide your group into teams allow each team to only have one to three balls. The only way a team member can move is if they are dribbling the ball.

Debriefing topics:
- What worked for you when playing?
- What didn't work?
- If there is something you could have done differently what was it? Why?

Lost In the Woods

(Khristins' Special)

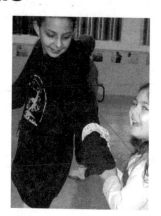

Sequence:
Initiative

Activity energy level:
High

Group size:
10 + (If you don't have an equal number of players allow one team to have an extra tree.)

Equipment needed:
2 Hula-hoops, green and yellow bandanas to divide the participants into two equally sized teams, a stopwatch or clock with a second hand, cones or extra bandanas to mark the center of the playing area

The objective:
To get to the other side and tie your bandana on to one of the tree's arms and get back to your side before the other team can tag you.

Playing the game:
Divide participants into two teams of equal size. If you have 7 people on each team three people on each team will be the Lost In the Woods people. The other four will be trees spread out on his or her team's side. Trees cannot move once they have picked where they want to stand. Trees are also not allowed to tag runners. A hula-hoop is placed on each side with the teams' bandanas placed in the middle. When the facilitator says "go" the Lost in the Woods players will need to run with one bandana at a time to the other side and tie it to a tree (**only loosely on an ankle or arm**). The runners must make it there and back without being tagged. If you are tagged after tying your bandana or your bandana is taken

down and doesn't count towards any points. If you are tagged before you tie the bandana on you must return to your side and place the bandana back in the hula-hoop and start across with another bandana. When five minutes is up the team with the most bandanas tied to the other team's trees wins.

Variations:
If a runner is tagged have them return to their side and become a tree by freeing another tree to run in their place. Allow each team member to only run once.

Debriefing Topics:
- How did you feel being a tree?
- How did you feel when you were tagged?
- What changes would you make if allowed to play again?
- What kind of game plan did your team have?

Puzzling

Sequence:
Group Games

Activity energy level:
Medium

Group size:
10+

Equipment needed:
1-2 Giant wood puzzles, bandanas for everyone, and one spot marker

The objective:
For the leader to communicate as effectively as possible to complete the puzzle in the least amount of time.

Playing the game:
First spread the giant puzzle pieces out around the room or play area. Gather group around and select a leader. Have the leader stand on the spot marker. This is where they must stand during the game. The leader's job is to direct the blindfolded people to the puzzle pieces, and bring them back to the front, where the pieces will be piled until they are all collected. The blindfolded people must work in pairs. This helps control movement of people and controls the puzzle pieces. Once all the pieces are collected, blindfolds can be removed and the puzzle may be put together.

Variations:
Have two teams and two puzzles. Keep teammates blindfolded while puzzle is being completed, but rotate leaders after each move.

Debriefing topics:
Depending on what is on your puzzle you can debrief about
the puzzle.
- How do you think it went?
- What worked?
- What did not work?
- Now that you have done this, what would you change?

***To make the puzzle you will need: 2 sheets of plywood, and
spray-paint. Cut the 2 sheets of plywood into puzzle pieces.
You will want to put the plywood side by side and draw out
your puzzle first. Or you can just use small squares with a
design painted on them. If you cut your pieces, make sure
pieces do not have any narrow areas. Those types of areas
break too easily. Color the wood pieces with different colored
spray paint. Use a multi-color design to make it a little easier.
After the background is drawn, spray-paint your pictures or
lettering.*

Knot Your Turn

Sequence:
Initiatives

Activity energy level:
Medium

Group size:
12+

Equipment needed:
Bandanas for everyone plus a long rope with knots tied in it about every 2-3 feet.

The objective:
To get the whole group to the end of the rope without having more than three people between each knot and without talking.

Playing the game:
Ask the participants get into groups of three. They will be moving along the rope with these people. There is a holding area located at the start of the long knotted rope. The holding area can be just a small circle made with another rope or an area taped off. The long knotted rope needs to be tied off the ground about waist high. If you can't tie the rope, you can have two people hold the ends of the rope so it is pulled tight to waist high. You will also need two people to act as referees and one to act as the conductor. The referees can move all along the playing area. Their job is to make sure only three people are touching a section of rope between each knot and call out the foul if more than three people are between the knots. If this happens, the small group removes their

blindfolds and goes back to the holding area where they must put their blindfolds back on and wait for the conductor to put them back onto the rope. The conductor is only allowed to take the group of three and put them on the rope and may not tell them when it is okay to move down the rope.

Variations:
You could set time limits for the entire group. If there is a mess up (foul) then the whole team has to go back to the beginning.

Debriefing topics:
- What made this a hard challenge?
- What did you learn about your team and your team's communication?
- How can you take the lessons learned in this game to life?

Chapter Three

Group Games

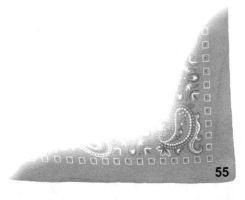

Number Tie Relay

Sequence:
Group Game

Activity energy level:
High

Group size:
8-20 if you do this with too many people it is hard to keep track of what number is being called

Equipment needed:
Two bandanas of different colors

The objective:
Complete the tie sequence before the other team to gain more players for your team.

Playing the game:
Divide the group in half. Have each group form a line facing the other team. Start them out with hands touching. While they are in this line, number off each facing pair. Ones, twos, threes, etc. Before moving your line make sure each player knows his or her number and who it is he or she will be competing against. Next have each line take 20 to 40 steps back so they are still in line with the person whose hands each was touching. Position yourself in the middle with one bandana tied on each wrist. (*Warning-take off your watch and tie the bandana loosely.*) Explain that when your number is called you need to run out and grab your team's bandana. Run to the other teams' side and tie it to someone's wrist that is standing in line. Then run back to your team and untie the bandana that was tied to their wrist. Take that bandana back to the other team and tie it to someone's ankle. Run back to

your team and retrieve your bandana off your teammate's ankle and tie it back to the center person's wrist. First one to complete this wins, the loser then joins the winner's team.

Variations:
Allow double knot tying or do not allow it. Change the sequence or add more to it. (e.g., Hop on one foot, crawl, or tie with eyes closed.)

Debriefing topics:
- How did you feel when you had to leave your team to go to the other side?
- If given the chance to play again could you come up with a better strategy?

Steal the Bandana

Sequence:
Group game

Activity energy level:
High

Group size:
10-25 any larger it is hard to control and remember what number is said

Equipment needed:
One bandana

The objective:
Steal the bandana and run back to your own side without being tagged.

Playing the game:
Split the group in half. Have the two groups line up facing the opposite team. The lines need to be about 20-40 feet apart. Have each team number off one through however many are on a team. Stand in the middle holding the bandana to the side and call out a number. The number called runs out to try to steal the bandana from the center and run to the safety of their own side. If the other team's players tag the person who is running with the bandana they do not win that round.

Variations:
Call two numbers to where the bandana can be passed between teammates.

Debriefing topics:
- What developments did you see throughout the game?
- What could have been done differently?

Are You the One

Sequence:
Group Game

Activity energy level:
Medium

Group size:
10+

Equipment needed:
Bandanas for everyone

The objective:
To find someone who is the same bandana color as you then as a team find the one and become one.

Playing the game:
Give each person a bandana. Set boundaries for playing the game. Show the group how to hold their hands up protecting themselves from running into things and each other. I call this "bumpers up!" (Thanks to Kenny Allen, MOSEY Outdoor Adventure Society for that term). Explain to the group that everyone will be blindfolded and will be in search for someone with the same color bandana as them. This is done by shaking hands and saying your color. Once you find a partner then you can search for "The One." The only way to find "The One" is to shake hands with people you bump into and ask, "Are you The One?" If someone asks you back "Are you The One?" You must keep looking. When you find The One and ask, "Are you The One?" The One will not answer. Join hands with The One and remain blindfolded.

*** *Chose The One after everyone is blindfolded.*

At some point and time The One will need to try to figure out how many people are still looking. If there are only three or fewer people still looking The One may signal to collect the others by saying, "Here we are!" If there are more than three people left looking when The One starts talking the challenge was not successfully completed and may be retired.

Variations:
Have only The One able to talk; everyone else must be silent after they find his or her pair. Don't have the group pair up before looking for The One.

Debriefing topics:
- What did it feel like to be The One?
- Now that most of you know what it feels like to be lost and looking for something what might you compare this to in everyday life?

Bandana Twister

Sequence:
Games

Activity energy level:
Medium to high

Group size:
12-24

Equipment needed:
Colored carpet circles (spots): 6 yellow, 6 red, 6 green, 6 blue, dice, spinner, bandanas, 3 pass chips for each group (optional)

The objective:
To keep your group and hold your positions. To not lose any players due to being blindfolded or having two falls.

Playing the game:
Set up the colored circle to look like a twister board. Break into groups of 6. Have each team stand in a different area next to the layout of colored circles.

Roll 1: Group One spins for a task. The group then rolls the dice. If the dice lands on 3 then 3 people from Group One must perform the task. (e.g., Right hand on red-3 people put their right hands on red while staying in contact with their group). Groups Two and Three must do the same.

Roll 2: If Group One rolls a 6, all 6 must move. The spinner might say "left hand on blue." All members of the group would put their left hands on blue but the three players who had their hands on red would have to leave their right hands on red.

The game is played in this fashion until someone falls. Once someone from a team falls a blindfold may be put on this person and play continued. This person cannot be a sideline supporter he or she is still part of the team and needs to be supported by the team. Play continues in this matter until one team has everyone blindfolded. The team with the most non-blindfolded players left wins.

Variations:
Do not tell the group they have to stay in contact. Give three pass/redo chips to each group so they can pass or start over on a hard maneuver.

Debriefing topics:
- What worked for your group?
- What did not work?
- Why was a plan so important before moving?
- Can this kind of planning help out in everyday problem solving? How or why not?

Who's Got My Tail

Sequence:
Group Game

Activity energy level:
High

Group size:
10+

Equipment needed:
One bandana for everyone

The objective:
Collect as many tails as possible

Playing the game:
Give each participant a bandana. Set boundaries for the game. Explain that the bandana is now a tail. It may be tucked into a back pocket or a waistband. It may not be tied to a belt loop. "That is cheating, and it rips the bandanas." Everyone is "it" and the object is to steal as many tails as you can. If your tail is stolen you are frozen. You can reach out and steal someone else's tail but you may not move your feet. If you steal a tail you can put it in your pocket and continue playing. If you are a lucky person who has many tails in their hand and your tail is taken then you may stop and put one of the tails that is in your hand into your pocket and continue to play. If you are a super nice person you can share your extra bandanas with your friends who are frozen.

Rules: 1) No stealing bandanas out of people's hands or when they are putting their tails on.

2) Tails must hang down out of pockets or waistbands. (Note: If you have someone whose pants are too big use a couple of bandanas to make a belt.

3) It is okay to give extra tails to friends if you choose.

4) If you go out of bounds you lose your tail.

5) If you drop a tail it becomes fair game.

Variations:
Each person can only collect two tails and if they get any more they have to give them to a person who has no tails.

Debriefing topics:
- How do caring, respect, responsibility, and honesty play a role in this activity?
- How can you use what we learned in this game at home, work, or school?

Partner Tail Tag

Sequence:
Group Games

Activity energy level:
High

Group size:
10+ must be an even number

Equipment needed:
Enough bandanas for everyone

The objective:
To collect as many tails as your team can

Playing the game:
Set the boundaries up for play. Have everyone pair up. Both players will need a bandana. Have the person in back tuck a bandana into their pocket or in their waistband with the bandana hanging down creating a tail. The back person then needs to put the blindfold on. The blindfolded person is in back the non-blindfolded person is in the front. The front person (the leader) needs to have the blindfolded tail person place his or her hands on their shoulders. You can only replace your pulled tail with tails that you have already pulled. Once all the tails you have are gone you become an obstacle. This is a game of elimination so once your team loses all their tails you stand back to back with hands outstretched to become obstacles in the playing field. You may pull tails but not put them back in to continue playing.

    <u>Rules:</u> 1) Stay in the boundaries (small playing field is better)
          2) Once you pull a tail just hang on to it.
          3) No running
          4) Do not leave your partner
          5) Only a non-blindfolded person can grab a tail.

Variations:
Have team add tails on as the others are pulled. This variation creates a longer game. Just make sure only one tail is pulled at a time.

Debriefing topics:
- How did feel to be the front person?
- How did it feel to be back person?
- Describe a time in your life when you might have felt like the front or back person?
- How did you handle these feeling?
- Would you do something different now?

Catch Me If You Can

Sequence:
Group Games

Activity energy level:
Medium to High

Group size:
10+

Equipment needed:
Bandanas for everyone, tape, 2-6 tennis balls or other small soft objects. (How many balls you use will depend on how large your group is.)

The objective:
Work together to score points for your team

Playing the game:
Split the group in half. Place a piece of tape down the center of the play area. The object of the game is to use the bandanas to catch and throw the balls across the line to the other team. There are two ways to score. One way to score is to toss a good toss to the other team and have them miss it. The other is to successfully catch a toss for your team. Your team looses a point for each bad toss to the other team. (This insures that each team receives a good toss to try to catch).

    Rules: 1) No tossing the ball too high or too low
            2) No flinging the ball
            3) Putting the bandana over your hand and
               catching the ball is illegal.
            4) Ball must be caught and thrown by only in
               the bandana
            5) You do not have to use every bandana

Give the teams about 1-2 minutes to plan. It is helpful to have a scoreboard and another person to help keep score.

Variations:
For players who are having problems tossing the ball appoint a person who serves, tosses the ball to the other team using their hand.

Debriefing topics:
- How did you determine who was to catch the ball?
- What was the best way to catch the ball?
- Does each of you feel your ideas were listened to?
- If yes, how did you manage that?
- If no, what could be changed so you can be heard?

Key Keeper

Sequence:
Group Game

Activity energy level:
Medium

Group size:
10+

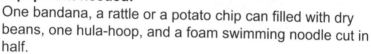

Equipment needed:
One bandana, a rattle or a potato chip can filled with dry beans, one hula-hoop, and a foam swimming noodle cut in half.

The objective:
To successfully steal the keys from the key keeper

Playing the game:
Form a circle with the participants. This is the playing area. Pick two people to be in the middle. You stand in the middle too. Place a hula-hoop in the center of your circle. Put your rattle or keys in the middle of the hoop. Have one person you select to be the key keeper or the guard. This person is blindfolded and stands on the outside of the ring. His/her job is to guard the keys or can from being stolen. The other person is sighted and is trying to steal the keys or can without being tagged. The circle is allowed to move in and out to change the size of the playing field. The circle's job is also to make sure the players stay inside the circle. The circle needs to make sure that they stay quite. You can play this as many times as you want.

Variations:
Have both people blindfolded. Allow the circle to talk and cheer

Debriefing topics:
- When you were blind how did you feel?
- What sounds did you hear?
- What sounds did you hear while you were trying to sneak in to take the keys?

Hobbits & Dragons

Sequence:
Group Games

Activity energy level:
High

Group size:
10+

Equipment needed:
Bandanas for everyone

The objective:
Work together to catch tails

Playing the game:
First you split the group into 2 teams. One team is the Dragons and the second team the Hobbits. The Dragon team lines up with arms on each other's shoulders and everyone, except the first person, is blindfolded. Each Hobbit has a bandana they will use as a tail. If a Dragon takes the Hobbits tail the Hobbit cannot move. If the Dragon gets to close and the Hobbit grabs one of the Dragon's tails, the Hobbit puts the tail back in and continues playing. When the Dragon gets a tail, everyone passes it back to the last person. The last person puts the tail in so now the Dragon has one more tail. There is no limit as to how many tails a Dragon can have.

Variations:
Partner up the Hobbits. If you have a large group you can use two Dragons. Have every other person in the Dragon line blindfolded in the Dragon line up.

Debriefing topics:
- How did it feel to be the leader (ask the head of the Dragon)?
- How did it feel being the tail of the Dragon?
- What did you think?

Fox in the Hole

Sequence:
Group Game

Activity energy level:
High

Group size:
12+

Equipment needed:
Depending on group size (one bandana per fox), (2-3) Hula-hoops, Raccoon Circles, or ropes. You also need a rope if you do not have a room with four walls.

The objective:
Working together to catch the fox

Playing the game:
Lay down the number of foxholes (determined by number of foxes plus 2 more). Chose foxes (for every 12 people you need 2 foxes) each foxhole can only hold one fox. Have the foxes stand in the "hole." The hunters pick a spot along the boundary. The hunters yell out "Fox in the Hole" and the fox must leave his hole and find a new hole. At that point, the hunters must try to tag the fox. If the fox makes it to another hole he than starts counting to five out loud so everyone can hear. If the fox counts to five before all hunters are back over the boundary than the hunters who didn't make it over the boundary are out. If a hunter pulls a tail from a fox he then becomes a fox and the fox becomes a hunter. The game is then played again.

Variations:
Change how many holes you have open. Give the hunters a chance to plan. Instead of having the hunter become a fox

just have the fox become a hunter (this works good for a large group with more than 3 foxes).

Debriefing topics:
- What was it like to be the fox?
- What was it like to be a hunter?
- Did you have a plan to catch the fox?
- If not, why? If so, what was your plan?

Team Tail Tag

Sequence:
Group Game

Activity energy level:
High

Group size:
12+

Equipment needed:
Bandanas for everyone but only of two colors so you can divide the group in half. You will also want to have about 5 – 10 extra bandanas of each color you are playing with.

The objective:
Working together to eliminate the other team.

Playing the game:
Once the group is divided into two groups each team needs to get a bandana of the same color for each player on their team. If you have 6 people on a team and 6 on the other you need 6 red bandanas for one team and 6 blue for the other. Each player is to get one bandana to be placed in their back pocket or back waist band so it hangs down almost to the back of the knees creating a tail. Each team is to work together to eliminate the other team. When a tail is pulled the person who lost the tail becomes frozen. The frozen person can still reach out and pivot trying to steal a bandana from someone. If you are on the blue team and pull a red bandana you will want to take it to the facilitator to trade it in for a blue bandana. That way if your tail is pulled you can replace it with your team colored tail. You can also share that extra tail with someone are your team who is frozen. The game is done when a team cannot move because the other team has pulled all tails. I also call game over if only one person from the other team is left with a tail.

Variations:
Do not allow teams to unfreeze his/her frozen teammates.
Only have three extra tails that can be traded in. Have the
teams play with the facilitator being the one who is to collect
tails. The team who turns in the most tails wins.

Debriefing topics:
- What plans did your team come up with?
- How did you decide what plan to use?
- Who was the leader of your group?
- What lessons did you learn from this game?
- How can you apply what you learned to everyday life?

Bamboozle

(Khristins' Special)

Sequence:
Group Game

Activity energy level:
High

Group size:
10+

Equipment needed:
Bandanas for each player. And 2 to 3 hula hoops. You will need more equipment if you have a large group.

The objective:
To catch the baboons.

Playing the game:
If playing with 10 people you will need 4 people to be the baboons, 4 people to be trees, and the other two to be baboon catchers. If you have an odd number, have that extra person be a tree. The baboons each have a tail. The baboons are trying to not get their tail pulled by a non-moving tree and to not be caught by a baboon catcher. Trees need to keep his/her feet firmly planted on the ground but they can still reach and sway to try to catch a tail. Each baboon catcher has a hula-hoop and is trying to hoop a baboon to catch them. If a baboon is caught by a baboon catcher then they become a tree, the catcher becomes a baboon and a tree becomes a catcher. If a tree grabs a tail he/she becomes a baboon and the baboon becomes a tree.

***Do not allow baboon catchers to throw the hula-hoop across the trees or room to catch a baboon.**

Variations:
Allow the trees to pivot on one foot. Give everyone a chance to be each thing at least once. Have the some of the trees be base for the baboons.

Debriefing topics:
- How did you feel when you were not able to move?
- How did it feel to be a baboon? How did it feel to be the catcher?
- Can you think of a time in your life when you felt the same way?
- If yes, how did you deal with that feeling?
- If not, can you think a situation in real life that would make someone feel this way?
- What could you do to make someone feel better who is feeling this way?

Monkey in the Middle

Sequence:
Group Game

Activity energy level:
Low - Medium

Group size:
12+

Equipment needed:
One bandana

The objective:
To escape from being the monkey in the middle.

Playing the game:
First have your group make a large circle and sit on the ground. The object is for the person in the middle to pick an animal for everyone in the group to make the sound of. First the person in the middle makes the animal sound. Next rest of the group makes the sound. The person in the middle needs to find the animal sound that sounds the most like his/hers. The only way for the Monkey in the Middle to escape the circle is to find a sound most like his/hers. The group is the judge of matching sounds.

Variations:
The group should each pick a different sound and then have the person in the middle escape through a certain sound named by the facilitator. Instead of animal sounds use rhythm. Have the person in the middle clap out a rhythm and then have someone in the group clap out the same rhythm. The person in the middle must figure out where the sound is coming from by pointing directly at the person making the sound.

Debriefing topics:
- What was it like to be in the middle?
- How did you find the sound you were looking for?
- Can you think of a time outside this activity where you might have felt like the Monkey in the Middle?
- How did you deal with feeling like that?
- Do you make others feel that way?

Sharp Shooter

Sequence:
Group Game

Activity energy level:
High

Group size:
12 – 20

Equipment needed:
One bandana for each pair of participants. Six – ten cones, six – ten tennis balls to set on cones and several kickball sized balls for throwing.

The objective:
To lead your partner to a ball to pick it up and throw it at the tennis balls on the cones.

Playing the game:
The cones should be set up in a line about 10 feet apart. Place the tennis balls on top of the cones. The throwable balls should be set up around the playing area. Have everyone pair up. Each pair is to get a blindfold. One person is blindfolded and the other is the leader. The leader stands behind the blindfolded person with his/her hands on their partner's shoulders. The job for the leader is to steer the blindfolded person to a throw able ball to pick it up. Then steer the blindfolded person to a spot ten feet from a cone to throw the ball at the tennis ball. The partner with the most tennis balls knocked down wins.

Variations:
Don't allow the leader to touch the person they are leading. Place tape or hula-hoops on the ground about ten feet from the cone so people have a base to throw from.

Debriefing topics:
- How did you feel being lead by another person?
- What was the main problem with being a leader?
- Now that you have done this once would you of changed anything about your leading style?
- How about changing your following style?
- Tell me about a time you felt this way in real life?
- How did you handle it?
- How can you use what we learned here today in the real world?

Fire Tag
(ESU Faculty Special)

Sequence:
Group Game

Activity energy level:
High

Group size:
12+

Equipment needed:
You should have 3 red bandanas for every 12 people playing this game.

The objective:
To learn Fire Safety and to put the fire out.

Playing the game:
Give a red bandana to three different people to tie onto his or her arm. They are now "it" and represent fire. Before someone who is it can tag anyone they must stop, drop, and roll. Once the "it" person has stopped dropped and rolled he or she can chase the other players. If you are tagged you must take the red bandana and tie it to your arm. You must stop, drop, and roll before you can tag another person. This game continues until you are sure your group gets the idea.

Variations:
Have the people who get tagged stop, drop, and roll and then becoming a partner with the original person who was it. This can represent how fast fire spreads.

You can also have a few black bandanas that represent smoke. Have a few people be smoke. The only way a person who is being chased by smoke can escape is to crawl low to the ground. Once a person crawls the smoke must go elsewhere.

Debriefing topics:
- What did you learn about fire?
- What should you to if you ever are caught on fire?
- What should you do if there is smoke in a room?

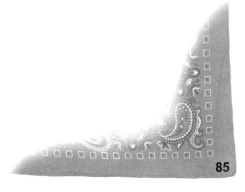

The Amazing Bandana Ball Race

Sequence:
Group Games

Activity energy level:
Medium to High

Group size:
20+

Equipment needed:
Bandanas for everyone, 2-6 tennis balls or other small soft objects. (How many balls you use will depend on how large your group is.)

The objective:
Work together to score points for your team

Playing the game:
Split the group into several teams. Then have each team form a circle with each player having a bandana. Ask each player hold their own bandana without touching the other players' bandanas or the other players. Place one ball in a bandana of one player in each team. When you say "GO", the ball is supposed to be tossed from one bandana to another until it is passed back to the beginning player. The only way to score is to successfully pass the ball around the circle to each person and back to the beginning player.

Rules: 1) No tossing the ball too high or too low
2) No flinging the ball

3) Putting the bandana over your hand like a glove and catching the ball is illegal.
4) The ball must be caught and thrown by only one bandana at a time
5) Absolutely no touching the ball with anything other than the bandana.

Give the teams about 2 minutes to plan. It is helpful to have a scoreboard and another person to help keep score.

Variations: The teams can also get into a straight line and pass the ball over their shoulders to each other. You can make the activity tougher by passing to every other player and when that is completed, toss to the players that were left out the first time around so that once everyone has caught the ball the team then scores.

Debriefing topics:
- What was the best way to catch the ball?
- Do each of you feel your ideas were listened to?
- If yes, how did you manage that?
- If no, what could be changed so you can be heard?

Capture the Flag with a Twist

Sequence:
Group Game

Activity energy level:
High

Group size:
12+

Equipment needed:
Bandanas for everyone plus one flag (to capture) per team

The objective:
To get the other team's flag and make it back to your side before your tail is swiped by the other team.

Playing the game:
Divide your group into equal teams. Establish sides of the playing area. Half court works well as a divider if playing inside a gym. If playing outside, cones work well for marking the center of the playing area. No pushing, going out of bounds, or tackling is allowed. The only way to "freeze" someone who is on your team's side of the field is to steal his or her tail. Instead of going to jail if you get your tail stolen, you are frozen. The object is for your team to capture the other side's flag and make it safely back to your team's side with out losing all your team's tails.

Variations:
Add time limits or make the person who captures the flag or a "frozen player" do a challenge before they are safe. Set up hula-hoops as jail that way instead of just being frozen when your tail is pulled, go to jail "inside the hula hoop" where you must stay until someone from your team rescues you or the game is over.

Debriefing topics:
- How does this game reflect the character traits?
- How can you take the lessons learned in this game to life?

Blind Red Light Green Light

Sequence:
Group Games

Activity energy level:
Medium

Group size:
12+

Equipment needed:
Bandanas for everyone and a large rope strung between trees or poles so that each section between the trees is equal.

The objective:
To get from one tree to the other before anyone else does.

Playing the game:
Participants need to be paired up. One person is the spotter and the other is blindfolded. Designate one end of each section to be the starting end. The blindfolded person stands there with one hand on the rope and the other hand in front of them to keep from running into things. The spotter is positioned down at the end of the section to make sure that their partner doesn't run into the end tree or move when they are not suppose to. During this game instead of yelling out "red light" or "green light" the facilitator or an extra participant uses something to make a subtle noise. The players are only allowed to move when they hear that noise. If they don't

stop moving when the sound stops, their partner must lead them back to the beginning where they must start again.

Variations:
When the blindfolded person gets to the end, they give the blindfold to their partner and the partner returns blindly to the end. Another variation would be to have the blindfolded person go down to the end, turn around, and go back. Make sure that the spotter is always stationed at the end of the rope where the blindfolded person is going.

Debriefing topics:
- What was most difficult for you as you made your way along the rope?
- Non-blindfolded persons, what problems did you run into while watching out for your partner?
- For both of you, what did you learn from this activity?
- How can you take what you learned out into the real world?

Audree's Relay Game

Sequence:
Group Game

Activity energy level:
High

Group size:
10+

Equipment needed:
One bandana for each player, 4 hula-hoops, and a rope

The objective:
To beat the other team at collecting bandanas

Playing the game:
First, place two hula-hoops at the far end of the playing field. They should be an equal distance from the starting area and about 10 feet apart. Each team should also get a hula-hoop at their starting point. In the far hula-hoops, place 7 to 10 bandanas in each hoop.

Split the group into two even teams. Have each player hold his bandana in his right hand. Then they need to form a line by holding on to someone else's bandana end with their left hand. This connects the lines forming a human chain with bandanas in between each person. One of the end players from each team should place one foot inside the hoop. This is the anchorperson. The other end is the retriever end. The whole group must line up behind the hula-hoops for the start of the game. When you say, "Go!" the group must move as a whole, staying connected, to retrieve bananas from their team's hoop across the room or playing field. When the retriever gets a bandana, they must deliver the bandana to the hoop where the anchorman is standing. Once at the hoop, the retriever becomes the anchorman and the anchorman becomes the retriever. They then go out to retrieve the next bandana. This continues until all bandanas have been brought back to the end hoop. If the team lets go of their bandanas as they are moving to retrieve bandanas the team must return that bandana and go back to the start position before trying again to retrieve a bandana.

Rules:
1) No stealing bandanas out of the other team's hoops.
2) No placing your team's bandanas in the other team's hoops.
3) If your team breaks the chain then you need be honest and try again.
4) The anchor's foot must remain in the hoop until the retriever is there to take their place. Otherwise, the team will be scrambled and all the bandanas will go back to the end bandana and the team must regroup and restart.

Variations:
Each person can collect two bandanas when retrieving bandanas. The retriever becomes the anchor and the anchor moves up the line but the second to the end becomes the retriever.

Debriefing topics:
- What did your team have problems with during this game?
- How could have your teamed changed things so it would have been easier?
- What made it possible for your team to succeed?
- How can you use those things in the real world?

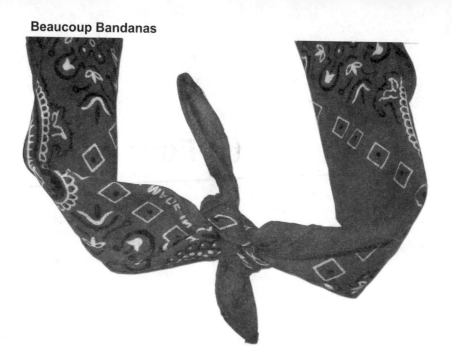

Chapter Four

Bandanas on the Ropes Course

Many times you will have repeat customers/participants on a ropes course. You will always want to continue to help those individuals challenge themselves and to grow. When I run into repeat customers I change things by adding bandanas. This book is in no way to be used to train you for proper use of either a ropes course or its elements. Please seek training by a certified ropes course instructor. Remember to always use proper spotting techniques. Do not ever blindfold someone who is uncomfortable with be blindfolded. Remember it is the participant's choice to take a challenge

Show Your Style

Sequence:
When your group first arrives

Activity energy level:
Low to Medium

Group size:
10+

Equipment needed:
Bandanas for everyone. You may want to plan how many groups you want. Provide only enough colors to fill each group. (e.g., 6 red, 7 yellow, 6 green).

The objective:
To create a feeling of belonging to a group. This is also a great icebreaker.

Playing the game:
Hand out bandanas to everyone. Tell them these are theirs for the day. (If you have bandanas with logos on them you may want the group to keep them). People need to display their bandanas on them with style.

Variations:
Pick groups first and have the group decide how their team will display their bandanas.

Debriefing topics:
- Why did you choose that style of displaying your bandana?
- How does the style you have describe your group?

Hook Up and Move

Sequence:
Ropes Course/Group Games

Activity energy level:
Low to Medium

Group size:
10+

Equipment needed:
Bandanas for everyone

The objective:
Move from one place to another hooked together

Playing the game:
Have the group hook up in one long connected chain.
Everyone must be hooked differently using only the bandanas.
You must also be able to walk while attached. Give the group
a few minutes to hook up. Check them to see they are all
hooked up differently. If they are, move on to next area.

Variations:
Every other person must use a bandana to hook up. Form a
circle instead of a line.

Debriefing topics:
- Who was the leader?
- How did you decide that person was to be the one to get you
all started?

Trust Formations

Sequence:
Ropes Course/Group Games

Activity energy level:
Low to Medium

Group size:
10+

Equipment needed:
Bandanas for everyone

The objective:
Form a shape while blindfolded.

Playing the game:
Get your group to gather around you and give them each a bandana. Once you get everyone blindfolded call out a shape and have the group form that shape. Next, ask them to take a certain number of steps in a certain direction holding that shape. Do this one more time. Pick someone in the group to be the next director. This is a fun one to do while moving from location to location.

Variations:
Do this as a stationery activity with a large group.
Split the group into teams and have everyone blindfold. Then call a shape out and have the teams form the shape. When a team is done they yell done. The facilitator then checks the shape. If it not completed the team must re-try. The first team with a good shape wins.

Debriefing topics:
- Did a leader emerge from your group?
- Was anyone in the group thinking of a better way but was afraid to speak out?
- What did it feel like to be the one in charge of the group? (Only ask if you have picked people to lead).

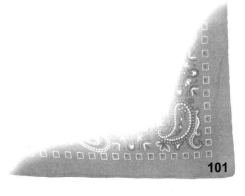

Three-Way Trust Walk

Sequence:
Ropes Course/Group Games

Activity energy level:
Medium

Group size:
12+

Equipment needed:
Bandanas for everyone

The objective:
Trust your partners to lead you through a path

Playing the game:
Split the group into groups of three. Have the groups of three stand so one of the people in their groups of three is in the middle with the other two on opposite sides of each other. (Example = (a) person on the left (c) center person (b) person on the right). The person in the middle is blindfolded the person on the left can see, but cannot talk or touch the person other than to stop them from walking into something. The person on the left can make voice sounds but cannot give commands like left, right, or stop. This person also cannot touch the blindfolded person. Switch around a few times and give each person a chance to be blindfolded.

Variations:
Have two people blindfolded with only one person to give verbal commands

Debriefing topics:
- Which was harder being unable to speak or being blindfolded? Why?
- How did you over come the challenges of this activity?

Circle Up/Wagon Wheel

Sequence:
Ropes Course

Activity energy level:
Low

Group size:
10+

Equipment needed:
Bandanas for everyone

The objective:
To get the group together so they can discuss their accomplishments

Playing the game:
This game is great way to bring a group together to discuss an incident or to recognize someone in their group for doing a great job. Have everyone hold their bandana in their right hand and grab onto someone's loose bandana end with their left. If you or the group needs to recognize someone they become a spoke of a wagon wheel. That person steps into the middle and grabs one bandana that is spread out between two people.

Variations:
Different shapes work well. Use this as a closing activity.

Debriefing topics:
- What did it feel like to be the first one in the circle?
- Look at your circle what does it look like?
- Why do you think everyone or almost everyone is in the circle?
- Should everyone be in the circle?

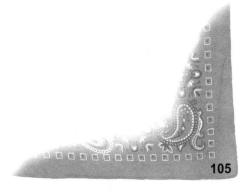

Mountain Tops With A Twist

Sequence:
Ropes Course/Group Game

Activity energy level:
Medium

Group size:
10-15

Equipment needed:
Mountain Tops, planks, and bandanas

The objective:
To maneuver across the planks to move from mountaintop to mountaintop.

Playing the game:
Split the group into small groups of three. Each group has one person blindfolded. Another is mute and can touch boards. The other can speak but cannot touch any boards. Put one blindfolded person on each platform. Put one mute person on platform and a speaking person on each plank (which cannot touch the ground). You should have 5 to 7 mountaintops and one 6-foot board and one 4-foot board. Set the mountain tops about 7 to 8 feet apart, enough so that one can be the exit out for the group. The correct way to traverse is putting the smaller board under the longer board. Have people stand on the shorter board to keep it from touching the ground and to hold up the longer board. Groups will need to figure out how to do this and how to do it without the wrong people touching the board.

Variations:
Place a blindfolded person on a platform by himself or herself or put a person on their own platform.

Debriefing topics:
- What was the hardest obstacle to overcome?
- Can you think of how some of the problems you ran into compare to everyday life?
- How can you use what you learned here outside in the real world?

Log Jam with Rocks

Sequence:
Ropes Course

Activity energy level:
Medium to High

Group size:
10-15

Equipment needed:
Log Jam and Bandanas

The objective:
To travel from one side of the "river" to the other using 3 logs and the "rocks".

Playing the game:
Set 3 to 5 square bandanas in different locations throughout the logjam. These will be the "rocks." The group is allowed to only use each rock once and only one person per rock. (If you need to make an exception to this for spotting purposes please do so). Do not set rocks too close to the end or the start because the group will use them, not the logs, to cross the river.

*** *I would not recommend ever using a blindfold as a consequence on this element.*

Variations:
Throw the hula-hoops where 3 people can stand. For an added twist, set a rope or more bandanas in the hoop that they can use if they want.

Debriefing topics:
- What worked?
- What did not work?
- Is there a time when you can think of that compares to this element?

Beaucoup Bandanas

As Consequence or Challenge

Sequence:
Ropes Course

Activity energy level:
Low to Medium

Group size:
Any

Equipment needed:
Different colored bandanas (Blue, Red, White, Orange, others will work)

Ideas:
Many people use bandanas as a consequence on the ropes course. Sometimes this creates too big of a challenge for people. So, I have started doing a few things differently. For example: When a person needs a challenge because they stepped off an obstacle or the board touched the ground. Instead of blindfolding them or hooking them to a partner try some of these suggestions.

Suggestions:
1) They are given a blue bandana to show they are the spokesperson for the next challenge.
2) Red bandanas mean you lose your voice.
3) White bandanas mean you get to share something with the group.
4) Orange bandanas are the safety bandanas. This means you step back and observe for safety violations. I use this one for two things. Either

someone just cannot do or does not want to do the obstacle. When an individual repeatedly jeopardizes the group's safety, or when someone just needs a minute to refocus.

Rainbow Climb on the Tower

Sequence:
Ropes Course

Activity energy level:
High

Group size:
10+

Equipment needed:
Red, Orange, Green, Blue, and Purple bandanas, tape

The objective:
To get the bandanas off the rocks and put them in the rainbow order from top to bottom.

Playing the game:
Set up the bandanas in different areas on the wall. The participants need to climb up and move one bandana at a time to line up the bandanas in rainbow order from top of the tower to the bottom.

Variations:
On a tower where two people can climb at once, having them construct a rainbow on the tower face by using bandanas. Time this event to make it a competition for the group.

Debriefing topics:
- What did you think?
- Did you feel you did well?
- Would you change anything about how you did this?

Goal Setting

Sequence:
Ropes Course

Activity energy level:
Medium

Group size:
Any

Equipment needed:
Bandanas of different colors and permanent markers

The objective:
To have participants set a goal, verbalize that goal, and write it on their bandana.

Playing the game:
Have each participant think about what he or she hopes to gain from the day's activities. It could be as simple as to learn everyone's name to as difficult as being able to climb and zip. At the end of the day, a goal wrap-up session can be held. For those who reached their goal, date and sign their bandana for them. If they did not meet their goal, help participants set a date by which to attain their goal.

Variations:
Have the teams set goals for their whole group instead of individually.

Debriefing topics:
- How did you decide what your goals should be?
- How do you feel about the goals you set?
- Did you set them to high or to low? If so, why?

Accomplishments

Sequence:
Ropes Course

Activity energy level:
Medium

Group size:
Any

Equipment needed:
Bandanas of different colors and permanent markers

The objective:
To recognize participant's accomplishments.

Playing the game:
Set up an idea of what each color of bandana will represent. For example Red can equal a brave heart, Yellow can be a great leader, Green a super problem solver, and Blue can be very trustworthy. At the end of the day, have facilitators hand out accomplishments to their team.

Variations:
Have the teams pick accomplishment bandanas for their teammates. At our camp we focus all our activities on character traits. We had out bandanas for our accomplishing or showing certain character traits. Red as caring, yellow as responsibility, green respect and blue honesty.

Debriefing topics:
- How did you feel receiving a bandana that color?
- Do you think you deserve that color? Why or Why not?

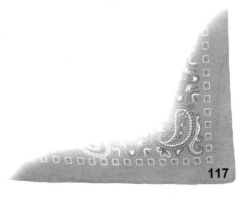

About The Author

Sara A. Shaw is the Executive Director of Camp Alexander near Emporia, Kansas and owner of K-S Recreation. (The K stands for Krueger, which is her maiden name, and the S stands for Shaw.)

She is also a Graduate Assistant at Emporia State University and is getting a Master's Degree in HPER (Health, Physical Education and Recreation). She has been involved with camps for over 15 years.

Sara has lived all her life in Emporia, Kansas. She is married with three children. One daughter was killed in a car wreck in 2003 (Tamara).

Other Bandana Ideas: